A Message to Garcia

T0145903

A MESSAGE TO GARCIA

And Treasured Wisdom

by Elbert Hubbard

Selected and Introduced
by Mitch Horowitz

*Discover the Simple, Life-Changing
Secret of this Motivational Classic—
Now in a Definitive Edition*

THE CONDENSED CLASSICS LIBRARY™

MEDIA

Published by Gildan Media LLC
aka G&D Media.
www.GandDmedia.com

A Message to Garcia was originally published in 1899
G&D Media Condensed Classics edition published 2018
Introduction copyright © 2016 by Mitch Horowitz

FIRST EDITION: 2018

Cover design by David Rheinhardt of Pyrographx

Interior design by Meghan Day Healey of Story Horse, LLC.

ISBN: 978-1-7225-0055-9

"We work to become, not to acquire."
—Elbert Hubbard

Contents

The Message
That Shook the World

This "literary trifle," as author Elbert Hubbard described *A Message to Garcia,* may be the most important piece of practical philosophy that you ever encounter.

I call Hubbard's writing "uncommon common-sense." This is because his work conveys truths that we should know, and perhaps innately know, but have forgotten amid the calls of modern commerce to turn everything into short-term profit and to expect that every experience deliver entertainment and pleasure.

Hubbard intended his short essay as a guiding light to illuminate, very simply, what separates the few exceptional people from the mass of mediocrity. His core truth is: "the hero is the man who does his work"—

thoroughly, energetically, and intelligently. The workplace hero does not make needless demands on others or require superfluous guidance and assistance; he does not deliver a job half-done or done only according to pro forma standards; but he *does his work* so that no one will have to fix it, embellish it, worry about it, or do it again.

Do not mistake this as a formula for worker-bee conformity. It is the opposite. Hubbard's credo, if you take it seriously and *act* on it, will show you what you're really capable of—and help you become a useful, constructive, and generative person.

Hubbard derived the title *A Message to Garcia* and his lesson from the experience of Lieutenant Andrew S. Rowan, an intelligence officer in US Army during the Spanish-American War. At the outset of the conflict in 1898, Rowan was ordered to deliver a vital US military message to General Calixto Garcia, the leader of a rebellion against Spanish rule of Cuba. All that was known of Garcia's whereabouts was that he was hunkered down at a jungle base in eastern Cuba. With little strategic briefing or material help from the US Army, Rowan succeeded in landing on the island, locating the rebel general, and delivering his "Message to Garcia," thus solidifying the US alliance with Cuban partisans, and leading to Spain's defeat in the war.

Hubbard wasn't making a political judgment about the war. He grew deeply critical of the intermingling of war and commerce in the years that immediately followed, as will be seen. Rather, Hubbard's focus was the character of Lieutenant Rowan: the young officer displayed independence of thought, resourcefulness, and tremendous determination, all of it applied with careful judgment and good sense. Those traits, Hubbard reasoned, are in alarmingly short supply in the lives of most men and women, who quickly vacillate from excitement to boredom, and often approach their work with apathy.

Hubbard first published his essay as a kind of space-filler in the March 1899 issue of his cultural magazine *The Philistine.* He said that he wrote it in just one hour after dinner one night. It was so minor a piece to him that he originally ran it with no headline. But the brief statement quickly gained national attention. Employers, managers, college presidents, and generals ordered copies and reprinted it, first by the thousands and eventually the millions. The essay became so popular that for many years the term "carry a message to Garcia" was slang for attempting a challenging task. *A Message to Garcia* got translated around the world and read by foreign armies and workforces. Parents gave copies to children who were starting college or entering working life. Enterprising clerks, with eyes on the corner office, gobbled up copies.

A Message to Garcia remained a mainstay of American success literature for close to fifty years. While the work's popularity is now nowhere near what it once was, it remains possible in the twenty-first century to find an employer here and there who still gives copies to new hires. It would be a help to the human situation if *all* employers handed it out today. Although the essay's message is chiefly about work and duty, its principles of personal enterprise and dedication are an excellent formula for peace at home: When you do things for people, rather than demand things from them (which can take subtle forms in the home environment), it demonstrates that you truly care about them. Every marriage therapist should hand out *A Message to Garcia*. Parents and children should receive it from family counselors. Prisoners working toward early release would benefit from it. So would law enforcement. Students who follow it would excel.

In short, there is almost no one today who wouldn't benefit from reading and following *A Message to Garcia*. Why is the pamphlet no longer widely read? Some readers may be put off by its unfamiliar historical references to the Spanish-American War. But these are easily illuminated, as I've attempted above.

There is one more reason why Garcia has fallen from its peak—and it involves a fair, but incomplete, criticism of the work. Hubbard's critics disparaged his essay for promoting servility and loyalty to unjust causes or employers. Some social writers saw Hubbard as a kind of false prophet to the workingman; someone who reinforced existing power structures and promulgated a message of complacency and know-thy-place toadyism. Hubbard reinforced this judgment by boasting that generals and industrialists had distributed his pamphlet by the millions. The pamphlet was given to Russian soldiers in the Tsar's army, and to every member of the early twentieth-century Japanese military. Both forces were known to commit acts of brutality and even atrocities. Hubbard's philosophy in *A Message to Garcia* can be taken amorally. But this is untrue of the man himself.

Although he had a flamboyant and somewhat media-catered personality, and although he betrayed instances of cloyingness toward industry titans, Hubbard's body of writing, as a social-reform journalist and an aphorist, loudly called for economic justice, legal protections for workers, and the criminalization of war profiteering. Hubbard helped expose child-labor abuses in Southern cotton mills—a social blight that chiefly profited mill owners in the North. His reportage led to some of America's first anti child-labor laws. He advocated for women's rights and suffrage. He experimented with voluntary communism and communal living. He thought it should be illegal to profit from the sale of military weaponry. He vociferously and vocally opposed World War One. This last commitment cost him his life. Hubbard and his second wife, Alice, a student of New Thought and a women's rights activist, were killed along with nearly 1,200 other civilians when a German U-boat torpedoed the British passenger liner the Lusitania in May 1915 off the Irish coast. The Hubbards were on a self-described peace mission to Europe to protest the war to the German Kaiser. Hubbard had hoped to gain a personal interview with the Kaiser (a reasonable possibility given Hubbard's fame at the time) and inveigh against the conflict.

"Big business has been to blame in this thing," Hubbard wrote of the war before his journey, ". . . let it not escape this truth—that no longer shall individuals be allowed to thrive by selling murder machines to the mob."

Seen in perspective, *A Message to Garcia* is an incomplete rendering of Hubbard's philosophy. Hubbard would have strengthened the work if he had infused it with a sense of his own moral purpose and discrimination. That said, Garcia is a *necessary* philosophy. Not just for ambitious employees, or for managers who are trying to overcome workplace apathy; but for artists, scholars, and those who work for social justice. People who see themselves as standing outside of traditional commerce often neglect the principles that Hubbard said make an individual effective and powerful. His methods—namely, throwing yourself into a task with absolute dedication, independence, and accountability—are as necessary for the artist and activist as for the executive and field commander. Artists who blow deadlines, activists who forget their pamphlets on the way to a rally, or union organizers who dither, hesitate, or put off needed tasks, benefit no one.

To fill some of the moral blanks Hubbard left in his great work, this edition of *A Message to Garcia* includes selections from some of his most stirring statements of moral philosophy. These passages flesh out Hubbard's full point of view. But be warned: Hubbard will frustrate any reader looking for surface consistency. At varying turns Hubbard celebrates capitalism, socialism, and anarchism. This isn't because he was fickle or erratic. Rather, it is because Hubbard had the capacity to see and embrace the highest good in philosophies that others might view as incompatible. In Hubbard's experience as a manufacturer, publisher, muckraker, and founder of a successful arts-and-crafts community, he proved his ability to combine tenets of all these out-looks. This was one of the marks of his greatness.

Although it is a short and brisk piece of writing, *A Message to Garcia* will take on new shades of meaning and provide new truths each time you examine it. Return to Hubbard's words again and again. Recommend them to those you love. It is one of the greatest gifts you could ever give or receive.

—Mitch Horowitz

A Message To Garcia

In all this Cuban business there is one man stands out on the horizon of my memory like Mars at perihelion.

When war broke out between Spain and the United States, it was very necessary to communicate quickly with the leader of the Insurgents. Garcia was somewhere in the mountain fastnesses of Cuba—no one knew where. No mail or telegraph message could reach him. The President must secure his co-operation, and quickly.

What to do!

Some one said to the President, "There is a fellow by the name of Rowan will find Garcia for you, if anybody can."

Rowan was sent for and was given a letter to be delivered to Garcia. How the "fellow by the name of Rowan" took the letter, sealed it up in an oilskin pouch, strapped it over his heart, in four days landed by night off the coast of Cuba from an open boat, disappeared into the jungle, and in three weeks came out on the other side of the Island, having traversed a hostile country on foot, and delivered his letter to Garcia—are things I have no special desire now to tell in detail. The point that I wish to make is this: McKinley gave Rowan a letter to be delivered to Garcia; Rowan took the letter and did not ask, "Where is he at?"

By the Eternal! there is a man whose form should be cast in deathless bronze and the statue placed in every college of the land. It is not book-learning young men need, nor instruction about this and that, but a stiffening of the vertebrae which will cause them to be loyal to a trust, to act promptly, concentrate their energies: do the thing—"Carry a message to Garcia."

General Garcia is dead now, but there are other Garcias. No man who has endeavored to carry out an enterprise where many hands were needed, but has been well-nigh appalled at times by the imbecility of the average man—the inability or unwillingness to concentrate on a thing and do it.

Slipshod assistance, foolish inattention, dowdy indifference, and half-hearted work seem the rule; and no man succeeds, unless by hook or crook or threat he forces or bribes other men to assist him; or mayhap, God in His goodness performs a miracle, and sends him an Angel of Light for an assistant.

You, reader, put this matter to a test: You are sitting now in your office—six clerks are within call. Summon any one and make this request: "Please look in the encyclopedia and make a brief memorandum for me concerning the life of Correggio."

Will the clerk quietly say, "Yes, sir," and go do the task?

On your life he will not. He will look at you out of a fishy eye and ask one or more of the following questions:

Who was he?

Which encyclopedia?

Where is the encyclopedia?

Was I hired for that?

Don't you mean Bismarck?

What's the matter with Charlie doing it?

Is he dead?

Is there any hurry?

Sha'n't I bring you the book and let you look it up yourself?

What do you want to know for?

And I will lay you ten to one that after you have answered the questions, and explained how to find the information, and why you want it, the clerk will go off and get one of the other clerks to help him try to find

Garcia—and then come back and tell you there is no such man. Of course I may lose my bet, but according to the Law of Average I will not. Now, if you are wise, you will not bother to explain to your "assistant" that Correggio is indexed under the C's, not in the K's, but you will smile very sweetly and say, "Never mind," and go look it up yourself. And this incapacity for independent action, this moral stupidity, this infirmity of the will, this unwillingness to cheerfully catch hold and lift—these are the things that put pure Socialism so far into the future. If men will not act for themselves, what will they do when the benefit of their effort is for all?

A first mate with knotted club seems necessary; and the dread of getting "the bounce" Saturday night holds many a worker to his place. Advertise for a stenographer, and nine out of ten who apply can neither spell nor punctuate—and do not think it necessary to.

Can such a one write a letter to Garcia?

"You see that bookkeeper," said a foreman to me in a large factory.

"Yes; what about him?"

"Well, he's a fine accountant, but if I'd send him up-town on an errand, he might accomplish the errand all right, and on the other hand, might stop at four saloons on the way, and when he got to Main Street would forget what he had been sent for."

Can such a man be entrusted to carry a message to Garcia?

We have recently been hearing much maudlin sympathy expressed for the "downtrodden denizens of the sweat-shop" and the "homeless wanderer searching for honest employment," and with it all often go many hard words for the men in power.

Nothing is said about the employer who grows old before his time in a vain attempt to get frowsy ne'er-do-wells to do intelligent work; and his long, patient striving with "help" that does nothing but loaf when his back is turned. In every store and factory there is a constant weeding-out process going on. The employer is continually sending away "help" that have shown their incapacity to further the interests of the business, and others are being taken on. No matter how good times are, this sorting continues: only if times are hard and work is scarce, the sorting is done finer—but out and forever out the incompetent and unworthy go. It is the survival of the fittest. Self-interest prompts every employer to keep the best—those who can carry a message to Garcia.

I know one man of really brilliant parts who has not the ability to manage a business of his own, and yet who is absolutely worthless to any one else, because he carries with him constantly the insane suspicion that his employer is oppressing, or intending to oppress, him. He can not give orders; and he will not receive them. Should a message be given him to take to Garcia, his answer would probably be, "Take it yourself!"

Tonight this man walks the streets looking for work, the wind whistling through his threadbare coat. No one who knows him dare employ him, for he is a regular firebrand of discontent. He is impervious to reason, and the only thing that can impress him is the toe of a thick-soled Number Nine boot.

Of course I know that one so morally deformed is no less to be pitied than a physical cripple; but in our pitying let us drop a tear, too, for the men who are striving to carry on a great enterprise, whose working hours are not limited by the whistle, and whose hair is fast turning white through the struggle to hold in line dowdy indifference, slipshod imbecility, and the heartless ingratitude which, but for their enterprise, would be both hungry and homeless.

Have I put the matter too strongly? Possibly I have; but when all the world has gone a-slumming I wish to speak a word of sympathy for the man who succeeds— the man who, against great odds, has directed the efforts of others, and having succeeded, finds there's nothing in it: nothing but bare board and clothes. I have carried a dinner-pail and worked for day's wages, and I have also been an employer of labor, and I know there is something to be said on both sides. There is no excellence, per se, in poverty; rags are no recommendation; and all employers are not rapacious and high-handed, any more than all poor men are virtuous. My heart goes out to the man who does his work when the "boss" is away, as well as when he is at home. And the man who, when given a letter for Garcia, quietly takes the missive, without asking any idiotic questions, and with no lurking intention of chucking it into the nearest sewer, or of doing aught else but deliver it, never gets "laid off," nor has to go on a strike for higher wages. Civilization is one long, anxious search for just such individuals. Anything such a man asks shall be granted. His kind is so rare that no employer can afford to let him go. He is wanted in every city, town and village—in every office, shop, store and factory. The world cries out for such: he is needed and needed badly—the man who can "Carry a Message to Garcia."

Uncommon Commonsense:
Passages by Elbert Hubbard

LIFE LIES IN THE QUEST

We need the colleges, but not for segregation, nor for noisy yells and sophomoric pride in smug futility of Greek-letter societies, with their senseless, soulless mummery.

Why not a workshop instead?

The university of the future will supply certain conditions of growth and these will be free to all who care to work for them, and all who care to work for them will be free to do so.

If a man will not work, neither shall he eat.

If a man will not work, neither shall he be educated.

In future, our children shall go to school—not be sent nor sentenced. Nothing is of any value to you except what you work for. Things given you and thrust upon you are forever alien to you—separate and apart, and will be molted very shortly.

That which is worth having is worth working for.

Education is not an acquisition, it is an achievement. Like liberty you must earn it, or you'll wander forever in the desert, a slave in spirit still.

—1904

HORSE SENSE

If you work for a man, in Heaven's name work for him. If he pays wages that supply you your bread and butter, work for him, speak well of him, think well of him, and stand by him, and stand by the institution he represents. I think if I worked for a man, I would work for him. I would not work for him a part of his time, but all of his time. I would give an undivided service or none. If put to the pinch, an ounce of loyalty is worth a pound of cleverness. If you must vilify, condemn, and eternally disparage, why, resign your position, and when you are outside, damn to your heart's content. But, I pray you, so long as you are a part of an institution, do not condemn it. Not that you will injure the institution—not that—but when you disparage the concern of which you are a part, you disparage yourself. And don't forget— "I forgot" won't do in business.

—Circa 1899

JESUS WAS AN ANARCHIST

An Anarchist is one who minds his own business. An Anarchist does not believe in sending warships across wide oceans to kill brown men, and lay waste rice fields, and burn the homes of people fighting for liberty. An Anarchist does not drive women with babes at their breasts and other women with babes unborn, children and old men into the jungle to be devoured by beasts or fever or fear, or die of hunger, homeless, unhoused and undone.

. . . I believe that brutality tends to defeat itself. Prize fighters die young, gourmands get the gout, hate hurts worse the man who nurses it, and all selfishness robs the mind of its divine insight, and cheats the soul that would know. Mind alone is eternal! He, watching over Israel, slumbers not nor sleeps. My faith is great: out of the transient darkness of the present the shadows will flee away, and Day will yet dawn.

. . . I am an Anarchist.

No man who believes in force and violence is an Anarchist. The true Anarchist decries all influences save those of love and reason. Ideas are his only arms.

Being an Anarchist I am also a Socialist. Socialism is the antithesis of Anarchy. One is the North Pole of Truth, the other the South. The Socialist believes in working for the good of all, while Anarchy is pure Individualism. I believe in every man working for the good of self; and in working for the good of self, he works for the good of all. To think, to see, to feel, to know; to deal justly; to bear all patiently; to act quietly; to speak cheerfully; to moderate one's voice—these things will bring you the highest good. They will bring you the love of the best, and the esteem of that Sacred Few, whose good opinion alone is worth cultivating. And further than this, it is the best way you can serve Society—live your life. The wise way to benefit humanity is to attend to your own affairs, and thus give other people an opportunity to look after theirs.

If there is any better way to teach virtue than by practicing it, I do not know it. Would you make men better—set them an example

—1901

An Educated Person

1. Man's education is never complete, and life and education should go hand in hand to the end.
2. By separating education from practical life society has inculcated the vicious belief that education is one thing and life another.

3. Five hours of intelligently directed work a day will supply ample board, lodging, and clothing to the adolescent student, male or female.

4. Five hours of manual labor will not only support the student, but it will add to his intellectual vigor and conduce to his better physical, mental and, spiritual development.

5. This work should be directly in the line of education, and part of the school curriculum.

6. No effort of life need be inutile, but all effort should be useful in order to satisfy the consciousness.

7. Somebody must do the work of the world. There is a certain amount of work to do, and the reason some people have to labor from daylight until dark is because others never work at all.

8. To do a certain amount of manual labor every day, should be accounted a privilege to every normal man and woman.

9. No person should be overworked.

10. All should do some work.

11. To work intelligently is education.

12. To abstain from useful work in order to get an education, is to get an education of the wrong kind, that is to say, a false education.

13. From fourteen years up, every normal individual can be self-supporting, and to be so is a God-given

privilege, conductive to the best mental, moral, and spiritual development.

14. The plan of examinations, in order to ascertain how much the pupil knows, does not reveal how much the pupil knows, causes much misery, is conducive to hypocrisy, and is like pulling up the plant to examine its roots. It further indicates that we have small faith in our methods.

15. People who have too much leisure consume more than they should, and do not produce enough.

16. To go to school for four years, or six, is no proof of excellence; any more than to fail in an examination is proof of incompetence.

17. The giving of degrees and diplomas to people who have done no useful things is puerile and absurd, since degrees so secured are no proof of competence, and tend to inflate the holder with the idea that he is some great one when, probably, he isn't.

18. All degrees should be honorary, and be given for meritorious service to society—that is, for doing something useful for somebody.

19. The walls of the old-time college are crumbling, and the University of the future will have around it no twelve-foot-high iron fence.

The chief error of the colleges lies in the fact that they have separated the world of culture from the world of work.

They have fostered the fallacy that one set of men should do the labor, and another set should have the education—that one should be ornamental and the other useful.

Then, to bolster their position, they have manufactured specious arguments trying to show that the professionals who supply truth and art to the poor people who have neither, are better than the folks who toil to feed and clothe the folks who make the arguments.

The fact is that the opportunities for education should be within the reach of every individual, not for the lucky few. Nature is opposed to monopolies and so she nips the selfish ambitions of your exclusively educated person and says, "Go to! get your education and be damned!"

And he often is.

Hence we get a condition approaching that which existed in the Fifteenth Century, when nobody was educated because the schools graduated only the top-heavy.

—1904

I BELIEVE

I believe in myself.

I believe in the goods I sell.

I believe in my colleagues and helpers.

I believe in the efficacy of printer's ink.

I believe in producers, creators, manufacturers, distributors, and in all the workers of the world who have a job and hold it down.

I believe that truth is an asset.

I believe that the first requisite in success is not to achieve a dollar but to confer a benefit, and that the reward will come automatically and usually as a matter of course.

I believe that the greatest word in the English language is "Sufficiency."

I believe that when I make a sale I must make a friend.

I believe that when I part with you I must do it in such a way that when you see me again you will be glad—and so will I.

I believe in the hands that work, in the brains that think, and in the hearts that love.

   —1912, adapted form Elbert Hubbard's *Credo*

About the Authors

Journalist ELBERT HUBBARD was born in Blooming-ton, Illinois, in 1856. A founder of the Arts and Crafts movement community Roycroft, in East Aurora, New York, Hubbard acted as publisher and editor of two popular cultural magazines, *The Philistine* and *The Fra*. Hubbard and his second wife Alice died aboard the British steamer the Lusitania in 1915, after it was torpedoed and sunk by a German submarine. He was en route to Europe, on a trip to encourage the end of World War One. Famous for his motivational writing and social-reform journalism, Hubbard's *A Message to Garcia* is one of the most widely read works in history.

MITCH HOROWITZ, who abridged and introduced this volume, is the PEN Award-winning author of books including *Occult America* and *The Miracle Club: How Thoughts Become Reality*. *The Washington Post* says Mitch "treats esoteric ideas and movements with an even-handed intellectual studiousness that is too often lost in today's raised-voice discussions." Follow him @MitchHorowitz.